Children of the
TLINGIT

THE WORLD'S CHILDREN

Children of the
TLINGIT

written and photographed by
FRANK STAUB

Carolrhoda Books, Inc./Minneapolis

For Pam, Dave, Graham, Elyse, Andy, and Sarah

The author and publisher wish to thank Lee D. Heinmiller, Sue Folletti, and John Marks for their help in the preparation of this book.

Text and photographs copyright © 1999 by Frank Staub
Additional photographs on page 15 (both) © Roby Littlefield
Map on page 7 by Laura Westlund © 1999 by Carolrhoda Books, Inc.

Carolrhoda Books, Inc., c/o The Lerner Publishing Group
241 First Avenue North, Minneapolis, MN 55401

Website address: www.lernerbooks.com

LIBRARY OF CONGRESS CATALOGING-IN-PUBLICATION DATA

Staub, Frank J.
    Children of the Tlingit / written and photographed by Frank Staub.
        p.   cm. — (The world's children)
    Includes index.
    Summary: Introduces the history, geography, and culture of the
Tlingit people in Southeast Alaska through the daily lives of
children who live there.
        ISBN 1–57505–333–0 (alk. paper)
    1. Tlingit children—Juvenile literature. 2. Tlingit Indians—
Juvenile literature. [1. Tlingit Indians. 2. Indians of North
America—Alaska. 3. Alaska—Social life and customs.] I. Title.
II. Series: World's children (Minneapolis, Minn.)
E99.T6S73 1999   98-20840
979.8'004972–dc21

Manufactured in the United States of America
1 2 3 4 5 6 – JR – 04 03 02 01 00 99

Above: *Crystal and her cousin Kimberly make a petroglyph rubbing. Crystal sells the rubbings to tourists for five dollars each.*
Right: *Ancient people carved this petroglyph near Wrangell.*

Southeastern Alaska has much to offer the people who live there. The waters are brimming with tasty fish. Many animals roam the forests. Plenty of rain causes the trees to grow big quickly. In the summer, the bushes are heavy with sweet berries. Temperatures are never hot. And although winters in southeastern Alaska are long, dark, and wet, they aren't very cold. Snow and ice are rarely a problem.

The first people to live in this misty paradise arrived about 10,000 years ago. Their ancestors probably came from Siberia (a part of Russia), across a narrow land bridge that once connected Asia with North America. With so much food and other natural resources in their new home, survival wasn't hard for these ancient people. But we know little about them. Practically all they left behind were designs called petroglyphs carved in rocks.

The Native Americans living in southeastern Alaska, also called Alaska's Panhandle, may have descended from petroglyph carvers. From Metlakatla to Yakutat, the Tlingit Indians, along with much smaller numbers of Haida and Tsimshian people, make up about 20 percent of the population.

Crystal is part Tlingit. She makes petroglyph rubbings in front of her grandmother's house in Wrangell. First she lays paper over the stony images. Then she rubs the paper with crumpled-up ferns until the petroglyph shows through.

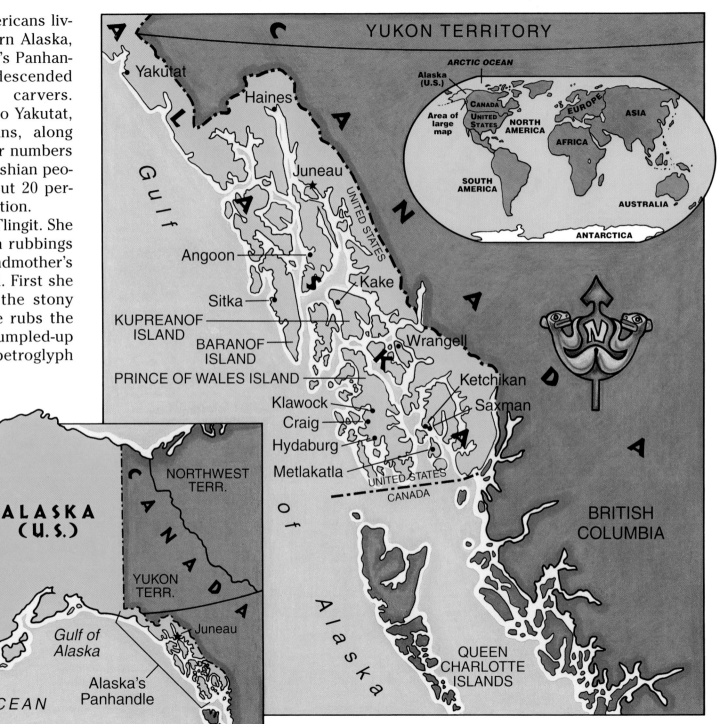

Walter sits beside a replica of a Russian blockhouse that once guarded against Tlingit attacks.

Sitka

Walter lives in Sitka, about 140 miles northwest of Wrangell on Baranof Island. Most of his ancestors were Tlingit. But his last name, Petrovich, is Russian. The Russians first came to western Alaska in 1741 and reached southeastern Alaska soon after that. They found many valuable furs in Alaska. So during the late 1700s and early 1800s, they set up settlements and made Sitka the capital of their Alaskan colony. But the land they had claimed in southeastern Alaska belonged to the Tlingit. For many years, the Tlingit fought the Russians to get their land back.

Ann Marie and Shaunte are at Saint Michael's, a replica of the original church built on this spot in the 1840s. The dome-shaped roof is typical of Orthodox churches.

During the Russian occupation, many Tlingit continued to follow their traditional beliefs. Many others converted to the Russian Orthodox religion. The number of Tlingit who call themselves Orthodox isn't as high as it used to be. But there are some Tlingit, like Ann Marie and her baby daughter Shaunte, who still follow the Orthodox faith. Some of the Orthodox Tlingit are members of Saint Michael's Orthodox Church in Sitka. Like Ann Marie and Shaunte, about 80 percent of those who attend Saint Michael's are Tlingit.

Richard and Tony catch tiny fish called bullheads (inset) in small pools of water along the shore. In school, they study these and other fish.

In 1867, Russia sold all of Alaska to the United States for 7.2 million dollars. But the native people who had lived in Alaska for thousands of years received nothing. Soon Americans started arriving by the hundreds. Among them were missionaries. Missionaries are people who try to convert others to their religion. Many Tlingit still practice Protestant Christian religions first brought to Alaska by Presbyterian and Salvation Army missionaries.

The missionaries saw that the Tlingit way of life was very different from their own. The Tlingit wore different clothes, ate different food, spoke a different language, performed different ceremonies, and held different spiritual beliefs. All of these differences led the missionaries to think that much of the Tlingit culture was evil. So with the help of the United States government, they convinced many Tlingit to stop practicing their traditions.

During the late 1800s and the early 1900s, missionaries forced large numbers of Tlingit children to attend boarding schools. At the schools, the children were taught how to be more like white people. Any student caught speaking an Indian language or practicing native traditions was punished, sometimes by a whipping. Over the years, religious organizations and the United States government have grown to accept and respect the Tlingit culture. Nearly all the boarding schools have shut down.

One boarding school was turned into a college, where Dionne is studying to be a teacher. Dionne is both Tlingit and Presbyterian. She has no hard feelings toward the Presbyterian Church, because it has publicly apologized for mistreating her people. Modern Presbyterian leaders encourage the Tlingit to practice their native culture.

11

It's the Fourth of July in the Tlingit village of Kake, located on Kupreanof Island. Most of the town is out on the main street celebrating. There are water-balloon-tossing contests, soda-pop-drinking matches, a tug-of-war, races, and fireworks. Rebecca is having an American flag painted on her cheek.

For some of Rebecca's Tlingit ancestors, the American flag was a painful reminder that they had been forced to abandon their traditional ways. Many Tlingit had also been angry that white settlers used Indian hunting and fishing areas without permission. Tlingit relations with the Americans, as with the Russians, were often violent. In 1869 the U.S. military attacked the Kake Tlingit and destroyed their village.

Rebecca's family has been part of the Kake Tlingit for many generations. After getting her face painted, she places second in the footrace for eight-year-old girls.

Eventually, the Kake Tlingit rebuilt their village near the spot where it had originally stood. In time the Tlingit and Americans accepted each other despite what had happened. During the early 1900s, the Kake Tlingit became the first Native Americans in southeastern Alaska to become U.S. citizens. About 700 people live in Kake; most are Tlingit.

Top: *Michael (in the blue shirt) drinks fast in a pop-drinking race.* Below: *The water-balloon-tossing competition is one of Kake's most popular Independence Day events.*

Blueberries (left) and
salmonberries (right)

Leann and Misty pick
salmonberries.

When the U.S. military destroyed the village of Kake in 1869, they also destroyed the people's winter food supply. In those days, the Tlingit collected almost all of their food during the summer to last the entire year. They caught fish, picked berries, gathered wild edible plants, and hunted game. They stored much of the food to eat during the winter. Obtaining food directly from nature is called subsistence.

Most modern Alaskan Indians shop at grocery stores. But many still depend on subsistence for some of their food. Leann and Misty are both part Tlingit. They help their families by picking blueberries and salmonberries in their hometown of Craig. Some of the berries will be made into pies and jam. Others will be canned or frozen and stored for the winter.

On this night, the girls take some of the berries to a potluck supper at the local Presbyterian church. Leann's mom says the supper reminds her of a potlatch feast. Potlatches are big Native American celebrations that recognize important events like births, deaths, and marriages. Potlatch activities include eating, dancing, singing, and storytelling. In the past, potlatches were usually held during the winter, when the people spent less time gathering food. A potlatch could last four or more days. The family who held the potlatch gave food, blankets, canoes, and other gifts to the guests. At modern potlatches, people might give coffee mugs, china, luggage, towels, artwork, or money.

Modern potlatches usually last just one day. Chuck and Dan (above) *perform a traditional dance at a potlach. Ed* (right) *watches a ceremony.*

During the mid-1900s, the Tlingit revived some of the native customs and crafts that the missionaries and U.S. government had tried to eliminate. One of those crafts was making clothing that the Tlingit call regalia. Like many Tlingit children, Leann and Misty wear regalia made by their mothers for special occasions, like dances and other celebrations.

Carving is another traditional craft practiced by the Tlingit, as well as by the Haida and the Tsimshian. Beautiful designs can be carved on copper and silver, but wood is most commonly used. The abundance of trees in southeastern Alaska makes wood a popular choice for carvings.

Leann and Misty wear regalia at Craig's Healing Heart Totem Pole. The totem pole was erected in memory of those who died from illegal drug use.

Skilled carvers create masks, rattles, spoons, bowls, and totem poles. Totem poles are logs carved with images of people and animals that illustrate events. Some totem poles tell a legend or family history. Others honor someone who died. Still others mark a special event like a birth or a hunter's brave deed. Totem poles may be only a few feet high or over a hundred. The missionaries thought the Tlingit worshiped totem poles as gods, so they persuaded the Tlingit to destroy many of these beautiful creations.

The Rock Oysterman Pole in Saxman recalls the story of a man who drowned when the shell of a giant oyster closed on his arm.

These totem poles are located in Saxman. During the 1800s, missionaries wrongly thought that totem poles were religious idols.

17

Warren and Wayne

Native craftspeople live throughout southeastern Alaska. Wayne is a Tlingit wood-carver in Haines. In his shop, Wayne works on a totem pole. But he takes some time to help his son, Warren, make a small canoe paddle. The paddle will be used as a wall decoration and as an accessory when Warren dances at potlatch ceremonies.

In Sitka, Tommy works on a mask while his son Jack practices carving. In the past, masks were worn by dancers during ceremonies to mark important life changes such as puberty, marriage, or death.

South of Sitka, near Ketchikan, Israel hollows out the back of a totem with his chainsaw to make it lighter and easier to move. His daughter Autumn enjoys the excitement of watching her dad work.

Jack practices carving by making circles on a board, while Tommy works on a mask.

John carves a toy canoe, while Lee works on a totem pole that will stand in front of a courthouse in Anchorage, Alaska.

Also near Ketchikan, in a village called Saxman, John carves a toy canoe while his dad, Lee, works on a large totem pole in the Haida style. Lee and John have both Haida and Tlingit ancestors. The Haida culture is similar to that of the Tlingit. Most Haida live south of the Tlingit in the Queen Charlotte Islands, located in British Columbia, or in Hydaburg, Alaska, located on Prince of Wales Island.

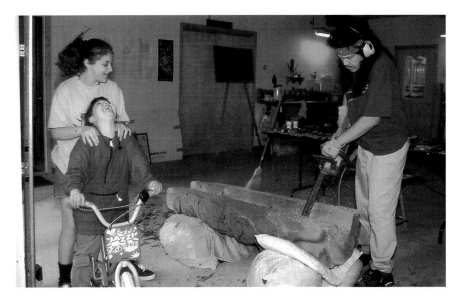

Israel enjoys time spent with his daughter Autumn and her stepsister Leigh. Chainsaws and other modern tools have made wood carving much easier.

After John finishes working on his canoe, he rides his bike to the home of his Haida cousins, Norman and Michael. Their dad, Norman Senior, is a construction worker. He has the day off and is getting ready to take his boat out to catch crabs. Michael will go with him.

John, Norman, and Michael are members of the Raven moiety. Every Tlingit or Haida child is born into one of two groups, or moieties—Raven or Eagle. In the old days, a person had to marry someone from the opposite moiety. Ravens married only Eagles, and Eagles married only Ravens. Over time, many Tlingit and Haida stopped following this tradition. But their children still adopt the moiety of their mother, not their father, just as they did in the past. If a child's mother is Eagle, the child will be Eagle. Raven mothers have only Raven children.

Michael, Norman Junior, and John watch Norman Senior prepare traps to catch crabs.

Above left and right: *The raven and the bald eagle are two of southeastern Alaska's most common birds.* Below: *Raven and Eagle crests decorate the Alaska Native Arts and Crafts Building in Juneau.*

Each moiety is divided into smaller groups called clans. Both moieties and clans are represented by symbols called crests. A crest is like an emblem. Crests may appear on totem poles, houses, and regalia. Most clan crests in the Eagle moiety portray meat-eating animals, such as the wolf and the killer whale. Raven clan crests include animals that eat little or no meat, like the beaver, the dog salmon, and the frog. Norman and Michael belong to the Loon clan. Clan, like moiety, is inherited from a person's mother.

Top: *Storm clouds loom over Metlakatla.* Above: *Tala, Mark, and Danielle take shelter from the storm at the basketball court.*

John has Tsimshian blood in addition to Haida and Tlingit. These three Indian nations are very similar. But unlike the Tlingit and the Haida, which have two moieties, Tsimshian society is divided into several groups, called phratries. Some are called Eagle, Raven, Wolf, and Killer Whale. Most Tsimshian live in a small area on the coast of British Columbia, Canada.

Tala, Mark, Danielle, and many other Tsimshian live in Metlakatla, Alaska's most southerly town. The three friends are hanging out at Metlakatla's outdoor basketball court, while one of the year's worst storms is raging. Fortunately, the court is protected by a roof. Rainstorms are common throughout southeastern Alaska, especially in winter. Due to the wet weather, Metlakatla schools have no baseball, football, soccer, or other outdoor sports teams.

Dan and Jerry wait for the storm to pass.

Jerry and Dan are both half Tsimshian. They got caught in the rainstorm on their way to a small Metlakatla grocery store to rent videos. Halfway to the store, their umbrella blew inside out. In another part of town, a roof blew off a house. The boys decide to stay at the store for a while to dry off and eat lunch.

Abundant rainfall in southeastern Alaska causes forests to grow tall and thick. Many houses are surrounded by trees. Cora, a Tlingit girl who lives in Kake, is swinging from a tree in the forest behind her house.

Later, Cora's brother Tom goes for a bike ride with his white friend Ian. Laws once kept southeastern Alaskan Indians and whites segregated, or apart. Indians weren't allowed to eat in the same restaurants or attend the same schools as whites. Native Americans weren't even allowed to vote.

Cora swings on a strong rope, which is used to haul up crab traps.

Tom and Ian

In 1912, the Indians of southeastern Alaska formed the Alaska Native Brotherhood (ANB) to fight for their political rights. During the next half century, the ANB helped win voting rights for Alaska Indians and convince white schools to accept Indian children. The ANB also helped get a law passed against segregation.

Much has changed since 1912. Whites, Tlingit, Haida, and Tsimshian work, play, and go to school side by side. They generally get along well. Indians and whites often marry and have children. Many southeastern Alaskan children are part white and part Indian. Scott is half Tlingit. He and his friend Willie agree that no one in their hometown of Klawock cares if a person is Indian or white.

Willie and Scott like to practice casting with their fishing rods at the school athletic field in their hometown of Klawock.

While his friend Haley watches, Gary works on a 20-foot canoe, which is almost identical to those used by his Tlingit ancestors.

The Tlingit, Haida, and Tsimshian once paddled canoes hundreds of miles along the coast to trade with each other and with other Indian nations. They also used canoes for fishing, hunting seals and sea otters, and traveling to distant potlatches and war sites. Some of the Haida canoes were up to 65 feet long. In Wrangell, Gary is making a canoe from a single cedar log. Canoe logs are taken from trees in sheltered valleys, where there is little wind that might crack the wood.

Families in southeastern Alaska travel short distances by car or truck. But there aren't many roads on the islands where people live. And the islands are usually too far from the mainland and from each other to build bridges. For traveling these longer distances, people use airplanes and ferryboats.

Dwight, Crystal, and Josh enjoy the wind on the ferry deck.

Dwight and Josh are taking a ferry with their mother and their cousin Crystal. They live in the Tlingit village of Angoon and are going to visit their father. He works in a gold mine near Juneau, Alaska's capital city. Their dad is away from his family for weeks at a time working. Unlike most southeastern Alaskan towns, Angoon has very few jobs to offer.

With so few jobs, many Angoon Tlingit have little money. Chelsea's family is having a food sale to raise money to help pay for medical bills.

Chelsea (right) stands with her friend Leanne at an Angoon community building, where Chelsea's family is having a food sale.

This replica of a traditional Tlingit clan longhouse is located at Totem Bight State Historical Park near Ketchikan.

In addition to logs for canoes and totem poles, trees once provided planks for the big rectangular longhouses that the Tlingit, the Haida, and the Tsimshian used to live in. Each house was made up of one big room. Up to 60 people, usually related, could live in one house. Each family had its own space. A cooking fire, located in the center of the house, kept them warm. Smoke escaped through an opening in the roof. Colorful crests often decorated the walls. Sometimes the big poles supporting the house were carved and painted like totem poles.

As American influence increased, more and more southeastern Alaskan Indians lived in smaller, single-family houses. Some of these early-1900s wood-frame houses still stand in Angoon. Many are named after a place or an event in a family's history. There are the Log Jam House, the Mountain Valley House, the End of the Trail House, the Bear House, and the Raven Bones House. Shauna and Angela's family rent the Killer Whale House.

Left: *Kenneth and Michael play basketball in front of one of Angoon's older houses.* Above: *Shauna and Angela sit on the porch of the Killer Whale House in Angoon.*

Ricky plays baseball with a neighbor in his front yard. He also likes to swim and to go fishing and boating with his uncle and grandfather.

Ricky lives in a modern house in Craig. His father is Tlingit and his mother is Aleut. The Aleuts are Native Americans who originally lived on the Aleutian Islands, located in western Alaska.

From his front yard, Ricky can see a hillside where loggers removed all the trees and other plants—a process called clear-cutting. Loggers cut down trees for lumber, paper, and other products. As in much of southeastern Alaska, many people in Craig make their living from commercial logging.

Clear-cutting is the easiest and least expensive way to log. But some people think there are too many clear-cuts. Not only do clear-cuts change the scenery, they also destroy the homes and food supply of many animals. New trees are usually planted after a clear-cut, so that there will be wood for the future. But it takes two or three hundred years for the new forest to mature. Unfortunately, the trees are usually cut down before they are even one hundred years old.

The Ketchikan Pulp Company uses forest trees to make paper.

A clear-cut above Craig

Isaac and Greig with a chinook

Greig, who is part Tlingit, goes fishing with his friend Isaac every chance he gets. The boys take turns using Isaac's fishing rod. Greig just caught a king salmon, also called a chinook.

In the past, the Tlingit's main food source was fish, especially salmon. They speared salmon with harpoons and caught them with wooden traps. But these methods are rarely used anymore. Instead, fish are taken with nets or fishing rods. In Kake, Annie watches her grandfather and uncle clean red salmon, also called sockeye, that they caught yesterday. Cleaning a fish means removing the head and internal organs.

Annie watches her grandfather and uncle clean red salmon, named for the color of its flesh.

Casandra cleans a dog salmon, or chum, near Sitka at a summer camp called Fish Camp. Long ago, the Tlingit used to set up temporary fishing camps in areas where salmon were easy to catch.

For one week, children at Fish Camp learn a little about Tlingit culture and food-gathering techniques. Any child is welcome, even if he or she has no Tlingit blood. Casandra has a few Tlingit relatives. But she is mainly Yupik Eskimo. Yupiks are the people of southwestern Alaska who speak Yupik.

A local fisher donated a few hundred dog salmon to Fish Camp. To make cleaning the fish easier, the children form a "slime line." Each child has a job, such as removing heads, scraping out internal organs, or cutting out bones. The children work at the water's edge so that any fish pieces that fall will be washed away. This helps keep hungry bears out of the camp.

Top left: *Casandra removes a salmon's internal organs.*
Above: *Children form a slime line at the water's edge.*

Brandon (center) helps carry trays of salmon to Ben (right) for stacking in the smokehouse.

Kendall hangs salmon above the campfire pit.

After the children at Fish Camp clean the fish, they learn a preserving method called smoking. Before freezers were invented, smoking was one of the few ways fish could be stored without spoiling. Besides preserving fish, smoking gives fish a delicious flavor.

To smoke the fish, Kendall hangs the larger salmon pieces on lines above a campfire. Brandon helps hand trays of smaller pieces to Herb for smoking in the smokehouse. A woodstove is attached to the outside of a smokehouse. Smoke from the woodstove is funneled through a chimney, which leads inside the smokehouse, filling the building with smoke. Many Tlingit families have smokehouses in their backyards.

Most of the salmon the children smoke will be donated to elders in Sitka. The campers learn the importance of treating elders with respect and listening to what they have to teach. At mealtimes, Ben, Paul, and the other elders who are helping out at Fish Camp are served first. Sometimes they tell the children about what life was like for the Tlingit in the past. The elders also tell Tlingit legends. According to one legend, Earth used to be dark all the time because a rich man kept the Sun, the Moon, and the stars in boxes. Raven tricked the man into thinking that he was the man's grandson. The man let Raven play with the boxes. Raven opened them and released the Sun, the Moon, and the stars. In doing so, he brought light to the world.

Paul tells stories as smoke pours from the smokehouse.

The elders at Fish Camp teach the children to use as much of the fish as possible. Salmon eggs can be boiled and eaten. Tlingit also eat the eggs of little fish called herring. Herring lay their eggs on plants in the shallow water near shore. Last March, some Sitka children placed small hemlock tree branches in the water for herring to lay their eggs on. The branches, with their coverings of sticky eggs, were then removed from the water and frozen until needed. To cook the eggs, Matt dips each branch into hot water for about 10 seconds. He knows that if he leaves the eggs in the water too long they will be tough and hard to chew.

Matt checks the herring eggs to make sure they aren't overcooked.

Left: *Charla removes nonedible plants from a bowl of wild parsley, wild peas, twisted stalk, goose tongue, spring beauty, violet, and other wild edible plants.* Above: *Robby's supper consists of salmon eggs and a salmon head. Children at Fish Camp must try everything. But if they don't like something, they're allowed to give it to someone else.*

The Tlingit have never been farmers. In the past, all their plant food came from the wild. At Fish Camp, children learn which wild plants are edible. Charla removes nonedible plants from a bowl of wild herbs. Venessa and Kayla do the same with a bowl of beach asparagus, which they gathered along the shores of Baranof Island. Some of these wild edible plants will be combined with the herring eggs in a salad.

Supper is made up of food prepared during the day. The Tlingit have enjoyed these foods for thousands of years. Although most of the campers have Tlingit blood, some of this traditional food is unfamiliar.

It's important to know how to get into an immersion suit quickly in an emergency. Matt helps Danielle try one on.

Roman scrapes a deerskin for a drum.

People who live in southeastern Alaska often catch fish from motorboats. So the children at Fish Camp learn how to use safety equipment on boats. They learn how to throw a life ring and how to set off flares to signal trouble. They also try on immersion suits. These bulky suits will keep them warm and dry if their boat sinks in the icy Alaskan waters.

Traditional Tlingit crafts are also taught at Fish Camp. Roman scrapes a deerskin for a drum. The drum will be painted with symbolic designs and used to make music for dancing.

The children also learn a few Tlingit words. When roll is called, they say *yaadoo,* meaning "present." And they learn to say *gunalcheesh* for "thank you." American missionaries discouraged Tlingit from speaking the Tlingit language. As a result, there are very few Tlingit left who can speak their native language.

Before Russians and Americans came to Alaska, the Tlingit had no writing system. Instead, they passed down information from generation to generation by telling stories, carving totem poles, and dancing. On the third night of Fish Camp, children and elders dress in traditional regalia. To the beat of drums, they perform Tlingit dances that the elders have taught them.

At Fish Camp, dancing is performed in Tlingit tradition.

Andrew, who is nine years old, makes money from dancing. He works part-time in his home village of Saxman as a dancer for the Cape Fox Dancers. The dancers entertain the many tourists who visit southeastern Alaska each summer. Andrew's grandmother taught him how to dance when he was just two years old.

Ben is a member of the Chilkat Dancers, who entertain tourists in Haines. During the summer, the Chilkat Dancers put on one or two shows a day, five days a week. In the lively Chilkat blanket dance, Ben wears a valuable Chilkat blanket. Chilkat blankets are made of mountain goat hair. Because of their thickness and complicated designs, it can take a year of hard work to weave just one Chilkat blanket. Very few Tlingit still know the fine art of Chilkat blanket weaving.

Left: *Andrew dances with the Cape Fox Dancers in Saxman.* Above: *Ben, Crystal, Logan, and Thia are four members of the Chilkat Dancers who are at least part Tlingit.*

Many of the other dancers wear button blankets. Button blankets are made by sewing buttons onto an ordinary blanket in the shape of a clan crest. Button blankets didn't appear among the Tlingit until they got buttons from white settlers during the 1800s.

Above left: Ben dances in a Chilkat blanket that is over one hundred years old and is worth more than twenty-five thousand dollars. Above: The pieces of copper, called "coppers," that decorate Thia's button blanket were once a sign of wealth among the Tlingit.

Later, Ben plays the "patient" in the shaman dance. Charlie Jimmie Senior plays the shaman. A shaman is a spiritual leader. Traditionally, Tlingits looked to a shaman for healing and guidance. The Tlingit believed everything in the natural world—people, rocks, trees, and animals—had souls or spirits. If someone got sick, it might have been because he or she had upset a spirit. One of the responsibilities of a shaman was to calm upset spirits. Once this was done, the sick person would start to get better. Shamanism is no longer practiced in southeastern Alaska.

In the shaman dance, Charlie chants while Ben plays the patient.

The Tlingit still respect nature. But when they get sick, they go to medical doctors. Many Tlingit work in medical fields. In addition, some Tlingit have jobs in sales, law, the airline industry, and a variety of other fields.

Donelle works in the Sealaska Building in Juneau. She owns part of the Sealaska Corporation as a shareholder. Sealaska is one of 13 corporations owned by Alaska's Native Americans. The corporations were made possible in 1971 by The Native Claims Settlement Act. The act returned some of the property rights the United States had taken from the Indians, Eskimos, and Aleuts. Any Tlingit, Haida, or Tsimshian born in Alaska before 1971 is automatically a Sealaska shareholder. This large corporation operates logging, fishing, construction, and other businesses throughout southeastern Alaska. Most of these businesses earn a lot of money, making Sealaska one of the most successful corporations in the state.

Juneau, Alaska's capital, is on the mainland. The large white building on the left is the Sealaska Building where Donelle works.

Alexa and James like to visit their mom, Donelle, at work. When Donelle is finished working, they usually go shopping or visit the library.

43

Left: *Loren pushes dog salmon down a chute so that they can be cleaned by other workers.* Bottom: *Sonja works at the radio station's control board.*

In addition to Sealaska, there are other smaller native-owned corporations in southeastern Alaska. While Sealaska operates throughout the Alaska Panhandle, these village corporations usually operate in just one town or on one island. Loren has a summer job in a fish-processing plant run by one of these village corporations, the Kake Tribal Corporation.

Sonja has a summer job, too. She works for a public radio station in Wrangell. Sonja does a variety of jobs at the station, including playing music as a disc jockey.

Winter days in southeastern Alaska are so short that it's hard to spend much time outside. In December and January, there may be just six hours of sunlight per day. So during the summer, when the days are long, the children go outside as much as they can. Richard and Timothy, who live in Saxman, like to play in the water during the summer. On this day, the air temperature is 78°F. That's the warmest it's been all year. But the water is still chilly.

Below: *Richard and Timothy wear special rubber socks to protect their feet from sharp shells that cover the rocks. Richard also wears a wet suit to keep him warm.*

In Angoon, a Tlingit girl has been fishing from the town's big dock. As the sun sets, she pulls in her line and heads for home. The days are getting shorter. Summer is drawing to a close. Soon the days will be very short and rainy. Then the time for fishing and swimming will be over for another year.

Pronunciation Guide

Aleut   AH-ley-oot

gunalcheesh   goo-nahl-CHEESH

Haida   HI-duh

Kake   CAKE or KUHCK

moiety   MOY-eh-tee

petroglyph   PEH-treh-glif

phratry   FRAY-tree

regalia   rih-GAYL-yah

shaman   SHAH-men

Tlingit   KLINK-it or THLEEN-git

Tsimshian   SIM-she-an or SIM-see-on or SHIM-shee-an

yaadoo   YAH-do

Yupik   YOO-pik

Index